SUBMARINER

The Thoughts of a
True American Mountain Man
(Volume V)

Preston Craig

Edited by Nicole Slavin

<u>*Author's Note*</u>

I would like to give my appreciation to the following people:

To my stunningly beautiful, as well as intelligent editor, Nicole. Thank you for all your immense patience for me as an author.

Thank you to Francesca for helping to bring my work to the page.

To Lucille for your undying support of my work.

To Emma Victoria – thank you for your kindness whenever I walk in a room.

To the podcast Love, Lies and a Side of Fries – thank you for having me on your incredible show!

1. Uncle Brad's pants caught fire at the annual wiener roast
   He won first prize.
   When Auntie was asked to describe the chain of events, and I quote, "He just went nuts."

---

2. Chet's nut roasting on an open fire.
   Well, get him out of the barrel
   Really. Christmas. Back to being Scrooge.
   Snow started early. Never took down the missing toe from last year.
   I practically had to blindfold the neighbor's kid just to get a kiss.
   Is bondage still legal in New York?
   Grandpa just got out - clubbed some deer for running over Grandma.
   She did survive but freaks out at the sound of sleigh bells.
   I sorta like Thanksgiving better.

---

3. March 15th, 44 B.C.

   Ban on concealed daggers.
   Very unpopular.
   Think I'll see a show.
   Maybe ask Brutus if he wants to come along.
   Full moon soon.
   All the crazies come out.
   March sucks.
   SPURINNA such a jerk.
   The days not over. Ha.

   J. Caesar

                                        Preston Craig

4. You may not be able to teach an old dog new tricks but
You can pat him on the head
Look into his eyes
Kiss him on his nose
So he knows
You love him

———————————————

5. Friendship- such a fragile word.

———————————————

6. On this date and day he went away
Alone, no one at his bed
No one holding his hand
No one to record his thoughts or what was said
Perhaps his mother or sister greeted his soul as he boarded the train
They had promised they would see each other again
Perhaps his favorite dog jumped on his lap
As he sat licking his face
Perhaps, more likely than not, his soiled sheets wrapped his lifeless form
Thrown in and buried in a wooden box, there to rot

———————————————

7. A young-un stumbled into camp
A runaway it seems
He still had his politeness about him
As far as survival skills he was pretty green
Around the fire they sat
The old bo not having much to say
The young-un asked "Ever been to the big house?"
"Yup" was the reply
"Five years at Dannemora. Kill't a fly"
"Hold on boy, I seez a skeeter"

8. Little Eddie Fischer gathered up the nerve
    To kiss her
    She pushed him away
    Gently
    Saying maybe someday.
    Neither forgot through the haze of growing
    Each knowing such thoughts would grow
    Their climb as a vine in time covering
    Choking that would deny their existence.

---

9. Dangerous Billy
    Looked kinda silly
    Wearing a pink over coat
    No one in their right mind was about to tell him so.
    Further down the road
    Off in a ditch
    A broken wagon lay under its heavy load
    And under the wheel lay old man Willie
    Still alive
    Twitch'in quite a bit
    As fate would have it
    A spider came up to Willie and sat beside him
    Neither one knew what to do
    They were besides themselves.

---

10. Love is always a step away from pain.

Preston Craig

11. The ice queen and her leather high boots
    Cape of black
    Quilted red liner
    Darkest raven hair
    Blood red painted toes
    Charcoal grey eyes
    A tongue that can touch your nose
    She walks through the night
    Her and lover Jack
    They stopped her early one year
    Froze my tomatoes
    Killed the squash
    Pumpkins turned mush
    April texted
    Said she will be here in'a bit
    Bringing her sister May
    Gonna kick some butt.

---

12. What a place to be stuck
    Haven't removed my boots in weeks
    The company clerk is buried behind me
    That shot was so close
    Rock and dirt thrown, hitting my face
    Gotta leave this trench of horrors
    Such a pretty plane, all red
    Three wings
    Don't that beat all?
    Wonder what's going on in his head as he stares at the ground.
    Halte an deinen Drüsen fest. Es ist ein langer Weg nach unten.

---

13. A tune was playing in my head
    The walk to the barn
    How quickly a full bottle drains empty
    Like the brain when dementia sets in
    I probably should of taken the tractor
    But I don't know where it is
    This cute woman cooks my meals
    Crawls in bed with me
    Have no idea
    She is always hugging and kissing
    Saying this is how it use to be
    I really don't remember the gag ball and bed post straps
    They always say get a second opinion.

---

14. Are you using me?
    You eat the best of food
    Come and go as you please
    I try to keep you warm on the coldest of days
    I never know if you want to stay
    Those bites
    That look
    Those green eyes
    Do cats have thighs?

15. I was to a place
    The other day
    Where I swore I'd not stay.
    I started to laugh.
    Touch myself, craved alcohol.
    Didn't matter bottle or can.
    Started to watch porn
    Driving with one hand
    To the beach to create castles
    In the sand
    I'd become a different man
    By reading one of Preston's Mountain..man..books
    Love to know their effect on women.

                                                        Preston Craig

16. I know of the birds and bees
    The bees sting your knees
    The birds crap all over your stuff.
    Now a tree is something to behold
    Even when old
    You still can hug em.

    Do they have nursery homes?

---

17. For months I've heard a rattle sound
    Ah...it's just in your head, I said.
    This morning taking my early pee
    I held a snake's skin.
    See?
    The shedded form was amongst the foundation rocks.
    Which means it's getting larger...

    Now a morning question?

        Which snake am I referring too?

            A) Common trouser
            B) Cotton mouth after a night of drinking
            C) Side winder
            D) Mississippi wrap around your neck
            E) What ??

---

18. Those eyes so dark
    Lips of pink.
    Not gloss I think
    I'm in trouble.
    Boots of leather with four inch heals
    Push up bra
    Makes it all so real.
    A voice that could calm a raging sea.

                                                      Preston Craig

Hidden string thong
Black, I think.
The women for me.
Thank Sis.

19.

 At the doctor's office for a simple check-up

I overheard Dr. J say

A year...maybe less

Definitely no more.

The woman, not a spring chicken,

Not a two-day old turkey after thanksgiving either

Presentable at any bar.

Our eyes fixed on each other's gaze.

I wondered if she were good in bed?

Could she read my mind?

I tried to erase such thoughts from my head.

Dr.J escorted her to the nurse's desk

Where she paid her bill.

I told the doctor I'd reschedule for another day.

"If you wait a sec Miss,

I'll walk you to your car.

Then your free to go your way."

That gaze again

Then a smile

"Sure, let's chat for awhile."

I found her more attractive than I first thought

SUBMARINER   Preston Craig

She seemed interested in everything I had done

Wanted to know my thoughts of the future

Things I wanted to do.

She told me of her grandma's farm

How we could live there together

As man and wife

Till death parted our love.

Here was a woman who wanted only happiness

On her remaining days.

How bad could it be??

Didn't want kids

Had money.

Vows were said

That night we were joined.

Two dogs and a cat in our bed

I'm not used to sharing a pillow or sleeping on my side.

Farm life began to agree with me.

Whenever we were to part we'd kiss

Like that day would be our last.

We never counted the months the hours or the day.

On coffee break with his staff

Dr. J glanced at the obituary page of the Daily Gazette.

"Please cancel my two morning appointments."

SUBMARINER   Preston Craig

20.

There was a man from Nantucket

Life was too heavy for his shoulders

So he just said screw this

Stripped himself bare

Shaved off all his hair

Started walking in the ocean deep.

It just so happened

A depressed shark was swimming by.

What the heck might be my last meal before I die.

Taste a bit like chicken.

21.

Missing his mouth

The shot of whiskey was wasted.

Although it gave him an excuse to wash his shirt.

The perfect white line down his throat

Where seconds ago was dirt.

Who cared?

Certainly not him.

He'd lost every ounce of self-respect.

If it weren't for the song

He wouldn't be able to spell it

Now to back track...

SUBMARINER   Preston Craig

22.

Are you having a good life here?

Do you wish you'd chosen better?

I wonder on our quiet times

I try to feed you well tho you are so fussy.

There are days when the cabin isn't as warm

When you nip me

Is there something you're trying to say?

Hey.

Who the heck knows what a cat thinks?

23.

One tooth

Two tooth

Three tooth

Gone

What went wrong?

I brush every day.

How'd that bald spot get there?

Used to be hair.

What's that you say? My hearing's perfect.

Please just repeat the part about my feet

Oh no, I'm not hungry.

Seems a dark cloud is above me

SUBMARINER   Preston Craig

Its not supposed to rain.

An hour ago it was sunny.

My leg does hurt now and then

You too?

24.

I was having such a great time being a jerk

Drinking alcohol as if it was just invented.

She showed me cleavage as an incentive

Sure, I followed her to the closet.

Then this guy jumps out.

Yep, I was in trouble.

At least I got his phone number.

25.

What a fine-looking day.

That bright moon.

Say where am I anyway?

    A) Twilight zone
    B) A minute before the bomb
    C) Nudist colony

26.

The:

a) Stone block
b) Mental block
c) Writer's block
d) Concrete block
e) Wooden block
f) Chopping block
g) Path blocked
h) Engine block
i) Block me baby
j) Just around the block
k) Chip off the old block
l) Butt plug

27.

I was up at a quarter to three
Usually awake at eight
I had a pee that would not wait.
While up
I raided the fridge
Yesterday's left overs didn't really appeal
Ah, the soda and rum
Steal the kid's juice to make a perfect meal.
Vacations are a wonderful thing
This family has been gone for over a week.

28.

Twiddle dee and me
Went to the State Fair
Being from New York
That's quite an event, wouldn't you agree?
First sight we saw
Were cows being milked.

Ordered two glasses of chocolate
I chugged mine
Twiddle used a straw.
Oh such sites we did see.

The rides were the best
It wasn't planned
On the Ferris wheel Twiddle held my hand.
Talk about laughter and fun
Just think - glad we are here early
Our day has just begun.
Such a fine sunny day
Even the rain stayed away
We would have kissed
We would have done a lot of things
If my heart could have let go
Love waited
But I was a no show.

29.

I knew a woman

Who would scrape mold off bread.

Toast the slice

Add butter and jam.

Sounds like us.

30.

They all hoped he wouldn't show

Every year it's the same

SUBMARINER   Preston Craig

You know

Brings his laundry to do

Dresses in clothes that need washed.

Of course, a bath you have to include

Minced meat pie, alcohol, and shrimp.

His favorite dishes.

Even the kids are sick of his sexual toned jokes

Still he insists it's all in fun

Surely not aimed at anyone.

The knock at the door makes all jump

Darn if it ain't:

A) Jesus
B) Mom's boyfriend
C) Dad's boyfriend
D) Auntie Jill who is in traction after being caught in a mountain slide on Blueberry Hill.
   (Guess that will learn her...thrill seeker)

31.

What a morning
What a sight
The moon was full
What a woman
Ain't waiting till afternoon
Getting my delight now
Darn dog, get off the bed
Cat, you get too
Be right back
Where is my other shoe?
Hold on now
We is gonna play hardware
I'm the nut and you're here for a screw
Alright, alright

SUBMARINER   Preston Craig

Thought I paid last night
Oh, that was then this is now
Anyhow
You take pennies?

32.

You got an issue
That needs a tissue.
A problem you can't solve
That needs to be resolved.
A boyfriend that might be the other way
It's hard to say
When it rains
It hurricanes.

33.

First words ever spoken by the Indians
When they laid eyes on the white man
"It's those Europeans
Keep 'em away from the tires."

34.

Why is it
Things you want to do in the summer
Never get done.
Things you don't want to do in the winter
Have to get done.
Really that's pretty lame
That thought won't even fill a page.
People buying this book
Will be in a rage.
Then about the refund.
Don't they know whiskey ain't cheap?

35.

Captains Log:
3rd of February 17 hundred 46
Rounded cape horn.
Three men over board
One got gored.
Ships surgeon says
That's gotta be painful.
The seas are rough
The crew are tough.
Not tough enough
They've seen the kraken.

February 4th 1746 ~
Only eleven of us survived
My first mate was the first
Then Willy then Billy
Then Nilley who just had a sex change
All succumbed
Ship surgeon says
That's gotta be painful

February 5th 1746 –
Set course 40 degrees lat. 10 longitude.
Storm has abated.
Seas are calm
The crew elated
Committed to the deep
Midshipmen Isiah Cambell died of hoof and mouth
He was a scurvy fellow
Always spoke when he should not have
Him and Nilley were bunk mates
The ships surgeon just sighed and shook his head.

February 6th 1746 ~
All is well at three bells
Sea calm
Easterly winds from the south
While scrubbing the poop deck
Crewman Addams slipped and fractured his neck

February 7th 1746 ~
Hope to find booty soon

                                                    Preston Craig

Stupid cat
War ship sighted
Will engage at morning light

February 8ᵗʰ 1746 ~
Well, nobody loves a pirate
Ship gone
Hanging on we spy an island
Six of us now
Somehow
We will survive
Choose sticks
One was picked
Ships surgeon says that's gotta be painful

36.

Ping pong came along
Was tired of being hit.
Suzy Q never knew
Annie Fanny was all to eager to board the cruise ship.

37.

Their eyes fixed
The stare
The sun's glare
Hot as a grease fire
Or Frank's hot sauce on your wiener.

New Mexico - 1878
Was it about a woman?
A spilt drink
A dealt hand of cards
Or Sally's house being closed.
The street was cleared
Not even the two combatants really knew.
Kids closed their eyes
The crack of thunder

A lightning strike
Not a movement could be detected.
Neither swayed or fell
Judge declared
He'd never seen such a sight
Looks like Sally's is open
Drinks on me.

38.

While hunting bear
I stumbled upon a native village.
Everyone ran as soon as they laid eyes on me
Something about my missing attire.
Chief says,
"You want to smokem pipe?"
I quickly replied
"I lean toward the female persuasion."

39.

As sick as he was
He lifted his body in pain.
"Hand me pen and paper
My last testament
Must be made"
As he handed his hospice nurse what he'd written
He died.
Somehow his stretcher bed rolled outside
From the fourth floor apartment dwelling.
How or why, no telling
As you might expect
His bed crashed in a tow away zone.
A truck showed up and removed him
Bone by bone
And that my friend is the end.

40.

Stow the fruit and bananas in the hold
Keep the rum caste in my quarters.
"Aye captain", as you say
"Shore leave for the men?"
"Sure, Number One.
We will pick up a new crew once set sail."
Skip and Do-Da decided to run away
They boarded a vessel
Bound for the straits.
"This will be different.", Do-Da exclaimed
"I hope we can relate."
The captain, a weathered soul
Well past thirty-eight says
"Welcome aboard mates!"
"Have a banana!"
Mighty kind of the old fellow, Do thought
"Have anything to wash it down?"
"Of course", says he
Close your eyes and count to three
We just sailed past the Virgin Islands.
"How far we going?" Skip asked.

41.

Poor little bear
His mom he searched for
Could not be found.
Nowhere.
All alone
He cried
His tears froze to his face.
Nothing could replace
Mom.
His poor heart about to break
A thorn in his foot didn't help his attitude much.
He took a taxi to 310 Honey Lane.
Dr. Benjamin Hive noticed his patient

Preston Craig

Bearly alive.
Immediately took him inside
And extracted the thorn from his paw.
It was then that the little bear spoke of his Ma.
How he had tried to find her
Doc said come to my waiting room
Snuggle up and keep warm on my new rug.

42.

The little mouse had it made
Living in its little house,
That was until the big freeze.
All his neighbors scurried in
Started eating his seeds.
With his winter's supply being eaten
In front of his eyes
What was he to do?
His little feet cold
The snow so deep
He went to wise old owl for advice
Being a mother of three a mouse was always welcome.
Not only was the little mouse's seed problem solved
His future college issues were also resolved.

43.

Come on Holly bring Jolly
Let's go for a Christmas cruise.
We have the money, honey.
Pick a spot
Whatever you choose.
Great, sees ya at eight
Say ain't this the ship that advertises half rates
And all the bananas you can eat?

                                                          Preston Craig

44.

Morning Grannie!
Breakfast smells mighty good.
Say where's Grandpa?
Sit down, Grandson
Pa and Uncle Jasper will be here shortly.
The stew needs to simmer a might more.
Sorta taste like chicken, don't it?
Donner Chronicles – 1834

45.

I think I just swallowed a wood chip
In my drink
Sooner or later
That will pass.

46.

I think the hardest times in a man's life
Are between 2:30 and 3am.

47.

We are supporting a mouse in this house
It comes and goes as it pleases
I'm going to get me a trap
And bait with different cheeses.
You know, I do have a cat.

48.

Train two miles away
Coming fast
Pressed against the track
My ear don't lie.

SUBMARINER   Preston Craig

Carries many blue coats
Some shoes and bras
Good place for ambush
Give big surprise
Take everything
Leave no one alive
Sioux vs Swamp Gulch express.
On that fateful day
The trussle bridge
Gave way.
Indians demanded payment for their losses.
Was then our hero
Came riding in
Dressed in buckskin, thin and mean.
Worse case of malpractice
He'd ever seen.
The whole case rested on the kitchen table
"Say I wear a 36 B
Any of them bras fit me?"
Sickened by the sight
Response from the jury
Took all night.
In the end it became clear
The verdict having been read
The color-blind judge said:
a)   I think I need a drink.
b)   They were Arapahos.
c)   Who was that buckskin lawyer?

49.

Me and some friends
Went camping
As we sometimes do
Up in the great Adirondacks where there are lakes galore.
Spring fed waters
Indian canoes on shore

Among the pines our female counterparts gathered wood.
I dug the latrine.
The forest animals seemed very friendly
Not one seemed mean.
That evening around the campfire where we sat
A little black and white bushy tailed cat
Boldly pranced among us.
Jim grabs him.
Starts tossing the poor creature in the air.
Thinking it fun.
Apparently, that was not
The proper thing to do.
For when the cat hit the ground
It ran to the nearest log
Lifted its tail as to say
"I'm out of here, you jerks."
It's smart
Always wise, bring the campers guide
Which on page two
Shows a picture of a skunk

50.

Up early with the crack of Dawn
The old man rolled over
Grabbed the "campers guide"
Seems skunks can be shape shifters.

51.

Ma and Pa were together
Seems like forever.
One day they
Had a fight.
Towards evening after supper
Pa suggested to Ma they have make-up sex
"Ok", Ma agreed
"Pa, grab my eye liner and wig."

                                    Preston Craig

52.

Either it is the smallest cat in the world

Or I just saw a mouse

Eating from his dish

Cabin rule #3 could not read any plainer.

This revolver of mine

Does it shoot high and to the left

Or low to the right?

BANG!

Now I have a frying pan

For a strainer

I swear mice can laugh.

53.

Older than dirt

Rusted by rain

Heart beat with hurt

Memories of pain

Start the damn bike up

Ride.

54.

I start to cry

When I hear our song.

Remember you saying goodbye

Well, it's been a year times ten

Some say you'll be back again.

Really, I say?

Throw an old dog a bone.

Chew on that awhile.

Let the juices flow

Snap the chain

Welded around your soul

Time to hunt.

55.

When your right

There's nothing left to say.

56.

Been stuck at post for almost a year

Who or what I'm watching for

I've no idea.

Now and then

Preston Craig

I see shadows among the trees

Hoping them friend

I wave, dance, shout,

Drop my pants.

Waiting for a sign of friendship.

I'll tell you what

They definitely were savages.

No time to close the gates,

No warning cry or even a "Can you wait?"

The first two I subdued

With super glue.

Four and five I shot

With my trusted '45.

Next, eight seen what I'd done

Wanted no part and they run.

Come morning revelry

First sergeant came to me

"Any problems the night past?"

"None at all, Sarge."

57.

Going to Albany Med for Christmas

To share fruit cake

With the patients

58.

Hail to the tree

Such a friend

It provides even after the end.

59.

He retreated to the hills

After prescribing the wrong pills.

True it cured her ills

It also numbed her from the waist down.

Hold on...hold on

I'll tell you more

Just need a mix

To fix my writing hand.

60.

Last night I had a dream

When I awoke

The grass was green.

Dandelions dotted the field

The smell of late spring

Turning to summer.

A gentle warm breeze of happiness

Filled my soul.

SUBMARINER   Preston Craig

Yep froze to death, I'd say

Pry that bottle from his hand

He must have had good taste

I drink that brand.

Why let it go to waste?

Really, check out the suit

Fancy tie

Size ten and a half boots

Now why would a man be setting on a bench

Waiting to die?

No idea, sir.

This is how we found him

He was half nuts.

60.

I saw Santa kissing Ma

Sis saw Grandpa stuffing the turkey

We stay away on holidays.

61.

You would think

After spending a week traveling the desert sands

Abdul would ask for a drink.

No sir-ree he asked for

A) a woman
B) a cat
C) a camel
D) a sheep
E) Thanksgiving dinner
F) all but (C) camels already been humped

62.

Sex spelled backwards is xes.

No spelled backwards is on.

Lana spelled backwards is anal.

Things to keep in mind if your dyslexic.

63.

Of course, I am a bum and alcoholic.

I farm and dig roots for food.

My blankets are of skins I've trapped.

Seems like forever

Since my last women stayed then left.

She believed in a bath.

Daily.

Imagine that.

                                    Preston Craig

64.

You can go back

Perhaps not to change

At least bend the rails.

65.

Squirrels hide their nuts

Then can't find them.

Some men know where theirs are

And refuse to dig them out.

66.

Man who leans on broken rail

At Niagara

Falls.

67.

A sober writer

........snooze.....yawn.........zzzzzzzzz

A writer drinking whiskey...

Hey a girl from Tennessee

Bumped into me.

I told her ha..ha..ha

I told her ha....ha....ha

To read my latest book

It's titled "Don't Look Now"

At the railway crossing

Pranksters changed the sign

To "park here"

Then held a sale on dented auto parts.

I think I'm gonna be horribly sick.

68.

Nights I can't sleep

I search the fridge for something to eat.

I awake tossing and turning

My eyes burning

Warm milk

Counting sheep.

69.

The rock rounded by water

Pocked by storm

A millennium old

Quite worn.

I gaze in the mirror thinking

Maybe a summer tan?

A little more hair?

Shock treatments to erase the memories

An extension down there.

70.

The women who never smiled

The personality of a toad

That got real old.

It wasn't that she was plain

Without a brain

Actually quite cute

With a perfect body

To boot.

A decree went throughout the land

To any man

Who could make the woman smile.

Thousands tried

They all spent awhile

Trying every trick they knew.

Nothing

You might ask

How this story ends?

To tell you the truth

The women packed up and moved to San Francisco

She makes flower hats.

71.

May I never forget

The kindness shown to me

The true meaning of friendship

To express it without measure.

72.

Me and the cat were just hanging out.

I started the conversation

What beautiful fur you have?

Those eyes of lime green.

Tail, long and sexy.

Love those whiskers too.

The cat said nothing.

73.

One year it rained

And rained

And rained.

I thought sell the plane

Build a boat

Not having much money

The built boat was kinda small

I did manage room for:

SUBMARINER   Preston Craig

2 worms

2 humming birds

2 tit mice

2 orange salamanders

Sure enough it began to rise

But that's another story

Ahab is describing:

    a) baking bread.
    b) the sun in the morning.
    c) temperature from winter to spring.
    d) a day on the Erie Canal.

74.

"Old no.7"
I could have chosen
"Old No.11"
But didn't.
Or even the one after "No.8"
True
Even "Old No.14 coming back from the glue factory
In powdered form
How about "Old number of hungry wolves
Waiting for you to fall asleep
And the camp fire to go out".

75.

Love is the stage before pain.

76.

The noodle factor-we
Closed for the company
Picnic

SUBMARINER   Preston Craig

Little Asian girl at the campsite
Sees a man in the bushes
"Ha ha, you we-we"
"No, I'm Hen-we"
"Oh", exclaims the child,
"Sar-we"
A very sunny day
All employees has a wonderful time.

77.

The little dog
Visited the hollow log
Practically everyday
Sticking his noses in
Sniffing the creatures who had been
There.
When satisfied all was clear
With no one around or near
Lifted his leg
And kicked the log down the hill.
As luck would have it
Dang naggett
But who was walking up the hill with a bucket
To fetch water for their aquarium
Yup
Wasn't a pretty sight.
To this day the old folks say
A marker should be placed
A song sung
In memory of that little dog
Whose collar tangled around that log
Was hung

Disclaimer
No animal was injured or hurt
In writing this epic tail.
(Applauses)

78.

The flash of intense light
Ground shattering rumble
No explication was needed
No broadcast announcement
Could have made the situation clearer.
The time for making wrong right.
Ended at 11:45
That night
The bedsheets tore
Restrains pulled loose from the wall
A collapsed ceiling
Debris as if a bomb had hit
Pilled so high
Rescue workers had to crawl
Betty Anne's first orgasm.

Preston Craig